donna hay

SIMPLE ESSENTIALS

pasta, rice + noodles

thank you

I have so many people to thank for helping with this book: Vanessa Pitsikas, for being a designer wise, composed and talented beyond her years; food editors Justine Poole, Steve Pearce and Jane Collings and their dedicated team of recipe testers for dishes that elicit oohs and aahs every time; copy editor Kirsty McKenzie for always asking the right questions; the amazing Con Poulos, talented Chris Court and all the other photographers whose images shine on every page; and, of course, to the *donna hay magazine* staff for being all-round superstars – your loyalty, creativity and professionalism help make donna hay a truly world-class brand. Many thanks must also be extended to Phil Barker at News Magazines; and to the team at HarperCollins. Thank you, thank you to friends old and new and my dear family. And to the men in my life: my wonderful sons Angus and Tom who make my heart soar, and my partner, Bill.

on the cover
front: spaghetti with tomatoes and capers, page 42
back: pancetta and sweet potato baked risotto, page 50

Fourth Estate

An imprint of HarperCollins*Publishers*

First published in Australia and New Zealand in 2008,
by Fourth Estate, an imprint of HarperCollins*Publishers*
HarperCollins*Publishers* Australia Pty Limited
Level 13, 201 Elizabeth Street, Sydney, NSW 2000, Australia.
ABN 36 009 913 517

HarperCollins*Publishers*
31 View Road, Glenfield, Auckland 10, New Zealand

Copyright © Donna Hay 2008. Design copyright © Donna Hay 2008
Photographs copyright © Con Poulos 2008 pages 1, 4, 7, 9, 10, 11, 12, 13, 14, 15, 16, 17, 18, 19 (left, middle), 23, 24, 25 (left), 27, 28 (right), 29, 33, 35, 36 (right), 37, 39, 41, 45, 49 (right), 51, 52 (right), 53, 55, 57, 59, 60 (right), 61, 65 (right), 67, 72, 73, 77, 80 (left), 81, 83, 85, 87, 94, 96; copyright © Chris Court cover, pages 19 (right), 20, 21, 25 (right), 28 (left), 31, 32, 40, 43, 47, 48, 49 (left), 52 (left), 56, 60 (left), 63, 65 (left), 68, 69, 75, 76, 79, 80 (right), back cover; copyright © David Matheson page 36 (left); copyright © Kirsten Strecker page 71.

Food Editors: Justine Poole, Steve Pearce, Jane Collings
Styling: Donna Hay, Justine Poole, Steve Pearce
Recipe testing: Miranda Farr
Designer: Vanessa Pitsikas
Copy Editor: Kirsty McKenzie
Consulting Art Director: Sarah Kavanagh

Reproduction by Graphic Print Group, South Australia
Produced in China by RR Donnelley on 157gsm Chinese Matt Art.
Printed in China.

The rights of Donna Hay and the photographers of this work have been asserted by them under the *Copyright Amendment (Moral Rights) Act (2000)*.

National Library of Australia Cataloguing-in-Publication data:
Hay, Donna.
Pasta, rice and noodles.
Includes index.
ISBN 978 0 7322 8579 1 (hbk.).
1. Cookery (Pasta). 2. Cookery (Rice).
I. Title. (Series : Simple essentials).
641.822

donna hay

SIMPLE ESSENTIALS

pasta, rice + noodles

FOURTH ESTATE

contents

introduction   6

basics   8

pasta   22

rice   46

noodles   66

glossary   88

conversion chart   91

index   92

introduction

If ever I need reminding just how lucky we are to be living in this culinary age, I need venture no further than my pantry. The range of rice on the shelves opens doors to the heady realm of the Asian kitchen and the exotic dishes of the Middle East. Meanwhile, the packets of noodles take me from China and Thailand to Vietnam, Malaysia and Japan, while the packages of pasta transport me to Italy, the heartland of generous hospitality. I invite you to join me on a fabulous food-based world tour with this selection from my favourite pasta, noodle and rice recipes. Treat your family and friends and bring them along for the ride. There's plenty of pleasure to be shared.

Donna

basics

The sheer range of pasta, rice and noodles now available in supermarkets is enough to strike fear in the hearts of even seasoned cooks. This section takes all the angst out of the process of selecting the right product for each recipe and the best way to prepare it. By following these simple tips and techniques, you'll never again suffer from aisle indecision or nagging doubts at the cooktop.

all about pasta

long pasta

It's no accident that spaghetti and its flat sibling, linguine, are the most popular pastas, as they match most sauces. Thick, flat shapes such as fettuccine, pappardelle and the hollow, tubular ziti and bucatini are best with robust, creamy, browned butter, meaty or rich tomato sauces. Thin pasta is great for thin or oily sauces, which coat each strand. Fine pasta such as angel hair (capelli d'angelo) or capellini is best with light sauces or in soups.

short pasta

Because short pasta is smaller and denser, it is ideal for chunky sauces containing tuna or vegetables such as broccoli and asparagus. Short pasta such as maccheroni and ditali is great in soups and broths. Round shapes such as orecchiette (ears), spirals such as fusilli, tubular penne and ridged rigatoni, are easily coated and are good for holding meaty, tomato or cheese-based sauces. They also make a great base for baked pasta.

sheet pasta

Sheet pasta, the foundation stone of layered dishes such as lasagne, is available fresh and dried. Dried comes in both instant and regular varieties. Regular lasagne sheets need to be boiled to soften before use, whereas instant can be used directly in the recipe. You may need a little extra sauce for instant sheets. Cannelloni are big hollow tubes suitable for filling and baking with sauces. A piping bag comes in handy when filling them.

fresh pasta

Fresh pasta cooks more quickly than dried, because of its high moisture content, so take care not to overcook it. As with most cooked pasta, the ideal serving state is *al dente*, an Italian term meaning slightly resistent to the bite. Fresh pasta also deteriorates rapidly, so check the use-by date and make sure that it looks and smells fresh. It's often a bit thicker than dried so it doesn't break during cooking, which gives a chewier texture than dried pasta.

all about rice

long-grain rice

Within the long-grain fragrant category there are many types of rice; which one you use depends on the nationality of food you are cooking and personal preference. Thai, or jasmine, rice has a delicate floral flavour, whereas Indian basmati is more aromatic. Unless specified, long-grain rice doesn't need to be rinsed before cooking. Regardless of how you cook your basmati rice, fluff it with a fork before serving. Salt destroys the delicate perfume.

risotto rice

Short- to medium-grain varieties, such as the traditional Italian arborio, are the best rice for risotto as they have a soft texture and chalky centre. The grains absorb a lot of liquid while retaining firmness, adhering together to become creamy. Other types of risotto rice include carnaroli, roma, baldo, padano, vialone nano and Calriso. Whichever rice you choose, don't rinse beforehand. The starchy coating gives the characteristic creaminess.

short-grain rice

Short-grain rice is a great standard for a multitude of dishes from baked rice puddings to sushi. Short-grain rice has enough starch for the grains to just cling together when cooked by the absorption method. Unlike long-grain varieties, short-grain rice has no distinct fragrance, making it more versatile. The moist sushi rice clings together, so is ideal for eating with chopsticks. The sticky quality also enables the rice to be moulded easily.

brown + wild rice

With only the inedible outer husk removed, the intact brown rice kernel is covered with layers of bran. It contains more nutrients and is higher in fibre than white rice. Brown rice takes longer to cook (and requires more water to do so) than white rice. It is light tan in colour, has a nutty flavour and a chewy texture. Wild rice is actually the long-grained black seed of a wild marsh grass. Be sure to wash it in several changes of water before cooking.

all about noodles

rice noodles

Made from ground rice and water, these noodles come in different widths, ranging from thin vermicelli to wide rice stick. Fresh noodles need to be soaked in a bowl of boiling water for 5 minutes before use; dried should be soaked for 10 minutes or boiled for 2 minutes before draining, rinsing and combining with other ingredients. Use as soon as possible after soaking. If preparing ahead, add a few drops of sesame oil to stop sticking.

wheat + egg noodles

These noodles, made from wheat flour sometimes enriched with egg, are available fresh and dried. They range from the humble instant or quick-cook variety and the Japanese ramen, popular in soups, to the fat, slippery hokkien of the Chinese and Malay kitchen. All varieties must be boiled or soaked before adding to the recipe. They are sometimes sold in packets as tight bundles or tangled cakes which need to be separated before use.

bean thread noodles

Variously called dried bean thread vermicelli, cellophane or glass noodles, these dried noodles are made from the starch of mung beans. They are most commonly sold as very fine strands tied tightly in bundles. Because the bundled noodles are hard to separate when dry, it is best to cut them with a pair of scissors. To cook, simply soak the noodles in boiling water until soft, then drain and rinse well. They are perfect in soups and salads.

soba noodles

Japanese noodles made from buckwheat and wheat flour, soba are greyish brown in colour and served in both hot soups and cold dishes. Cold soba are traditionally served on a woven bamboo plate or *zaru*. About the thickness of spaghetti, soba need to be cooked in boiling water before being added to the dish. Variants include mugi soba, flavoured with mugwort, hegi soba, containing seaweed, and cha soba, made with green tea.

cooking essentials

cooking dry pasta

Place a large pot of well-salted water, covered with a lid, over high heat until the water boils. Apart from adding flavour, salt increases the boiling point and speeds up the cooking time. Add the pasta and stir to stop the strands from sticking together. It's important to keep the water boiling, so replace the lid until the water re-boils. Stir the pasta again and cook until al dente. Drain. Allow about 100g (3½ oz) of dry pasta per person.

cooking fresh pasta

The only secret to cooking any type of pasta is to have plenty of rapidly boiling water in a large pan. Adding oil to the water won't prevent the pasta from sticking together, as it just floats on the surface and, if anything, encourages the sauce to roll off the pasta. The method for cooking fresh pasta is the same as dry but the cooking time is shorter. It's also easy to overcook, so test it frequently. Allow about 100g (3½ oz) of fresh pasta per person.

cooking dry noodles

Thin dried noodles, such as bean thread noodles and rice vermicelli, only need to be soaked in boiling water until they are tender before adding to salads, soups and stir-fries. Thicker rice or wheat and egg noodles need to be cooked in a saucepan of boiling water over heat for 3–4 minutes to make them tender. They can then be added to soups, stir-fried in oil or directly into the sauce to ensure good absorption of the flavours.

cooking fresh noodles

Fresh rice or wheat and egg noodles are available from the refrigerated section of most supermarkets and come in a range of widths and thicknesses. If they're vacuum-wrapped, remove the wrapping and stand the noodles in boiling water to separate them before cooking as specified by the recipe. When stir-frying some noodles, you will need to use 2–3 tablespoons of oil, so that they won't stick together or clump in a gluggy mass.

basic rice

Don't be daunted by having to cook rice. Boiling rice in an open pan may be a bit hit and miss, but if you follow these simple steps for the absorption method, you'll make perfect non-gluggy rice every time.

the correct balance

When you use the absorption method, the rice is cooked in a volume of water that will be completely absorbed during the cooking process. It won't need draining and there's no risk of ending up with a sludgy mess that's taken up too much water. You'll need 1⅔ cups (415ml/13¼ fl oz) of water to cook 1 cup of long-grain rice and 2⅔ cups (660ml/21 fl oz) of water to cook 1 cup of brown rice. Place the rice and water in a small saucepan bring gently to the boil over medium heat. There is no need to cover the pan at this stage.

the heat is on

Reduce the heat and simmer the rice for 10–12 minutes, or until tunnels form in the rice and the water is almost completely absorbed. Turn off the heat, cover the saucepan with a tight-fitting lid and stand it, without stirring, for 20 minutes for long-grain rice and 40 minutes for brown rice. The cooking process will be completed by steaming during this standing time. After the specified time, remove the lid and taste test. If it's still not al dente, replace the lid on the pan and rest for another 5–10 minutes.

perfect match

When short-grain and jasmine rice are cooked by the absorption method, the grains stick together slightly, which makes them easier to eat with chopsticks and perfect for taking up the sauces that accompany Thai and Malay curries and Asian stir-fries. Basmati rice is the exception, as it has a low amount of starch, so even when it is cooked by the absorption method the grains remain separate, making it the ideal partner for Indian dishes. For extra fluffy basmati rice, stir through with a fork before serving.

stirred risotto

Mastering the basic risotto-making technique is a passport to a whole new world of culinary pleasure. Don't be deterred by the continuous stirring – the end more than justifies the means.

getting started

For a risotto to serve 4, you'll need: 6 cups (1.5 litres/48 fl oz) good-quality chicken or vegetable stock, 20g butter, 1 tablespoon olive oil, 1 chopped onion, 2 cups arborio or other risotto rice (see page 12), 1 cup finely grated parmesan cheese, 20g extra butter, sea salt and cracked black pepper. Keep the stock at a constant simmer, but don't let the temperature get too high or you could use all the stock before the risotto is cooked. If the stock is running low, add some boiling water to the remaining spoonfuls of stock in the pan.

creating a stir

Place the stock in a saucepan over medium heat. Cover and bring to a slow simmer. Heat a large saucepan over medium heat, add the butter, oil and onion and cook for 6 minutes or until the onion is soft and golden. Add the rice to the onion mixture, stirring for 2 minutes or until the grains are translucent and coated with butter and oil. Add the hot stock to the rice 1 cup (250ml/8 fl oz) at a time, stirring continuously until each cup of stock is absorbed and the rice is al dente. This will take approximately 20–25 minutes.

the big finish

Stir through the parmesan, extra butter, salt and pepper and serve immediately. This will help to guarantee the smooth and creamy finish you want. Perfectly cooked risotto should sit in a creamy broth – it shouldn't be cooked to a dry mass. You can add any number of flavourings in the final minutes of cooking. Thinly sliced fresh mushrooms or reconstituted dried mushrooms such as porcini and their soaking liquid is one classic example. Smoked salmon strips, chopped dill and lemon zest is another tempting variation.

baked risotto

Did you know you can make a sensational risotto without all that tedious standing and stirring over a hot stove? It's easy. Follow these simple steps for angst-free, fail-safe risotto every time.

before you start

For a risotto to serve 4, you will need: 2 cups carnaroli or other risotto rice, 6 cups (1.5 litres/48 fl oz) good-quality chicken or vegetable stock, 1 cup finely grated parmesan cheese, 40g (1½ oz) unsalted butter, sea salt and cracked black pepper. Use good-quality risotto rice and either home-made or, if you don't have time to make it, the best store-bought stock you can find. Baked risotto works better if carnaroli rice is used rather than arborio as the extra starch on the surface of the grain gives a creamier finish.

into the oven

Preheat the oven to 180°C (350°F). Place the rice and stock in a 22 x 30cm (8½ x 12 in) 10 cup (2.5 litre/80 fl oz) capacity baking dish and stir well. Cover the dish tightly with a lid or aluminium (aluminum) foil and bake for 40 minutes or until most of the stock is absorbed and the rice is al dente. Take the dish from the oven and remove the lid. At the end of cooking time the risotto will still be quite liquid. To develop the creamy starch and thicken the consistency of the risotto, you will need to stir the rice for 3–4 minutes.

finishing touches

Stir through the parmesan, butter, salt and pepper. Gently stir through any other ingredients, as over-stirring will cause the risotto to become mushy instead of al dente. Lemon juice and chopped dill go well with fish, crispy pancetta or proscuitto will add a rich and salty edge. For best results, serve risotto immediately. If you want to reheat leftover risotto on the stove top or in the microwave, gradually add a little more stock and stir through gently. Leftovers can also be turned into sensational pan-fried risotto cakes.

sushi rice

Sushi, once a delicacy made only by master Japanese chefs, is now at home in your kitchen. So long as you start with proper sushi rice, it really is easy to make – you don't even need a bamboo rolling mat.

sushi basics

Sushi is a bite-sized Japanese snack comprising sushi rice with raw or cooked fish or shellfish, vegetables, omelette and seaweed. Sushi rice can be moulded into lots of different shapes, so don't be constrained by the traditional roll form. To make 4 cups of basic sushi rice, you will need: 1⅔ cups sushi rice, 1¾ cups (375ml/12 fl oz) water, ¼ cup (60ml/2 fl oz) rice wine vinegar, 2½ tablespoons sugar and ½ teaspoon table salt. Place the rice in a colander and rinse under cold running water for 5 minutes.

cooking sushi rice

Transfer the rice to a small saucepan, add the water. Cover, bring to the boil and cook for 10 minutes. Reduce the heat and simmer for a further 10 minutes or until most of the water is absorbed. Remove from the heat and stand, covered, for 10 minutes. Combine the vinegar, sugar and salt. Spread the cooked rice over the base of a large flat, non-metallic, shallow dish and sprinkle with the vinegar mixture. Stir with a spatula for 5 minutes or until cool to touch. This is to stop it clumping. The rice should be sticky, but not gluggy.

variations on a theme

Sushi comes in many different shapes and sizes. There are small oblongs or squares of rice with wasabi and thin slices of fish on top wrapped in seaweed, called nigiri sushi. Most common ready-made sushi from sushi vendors are the thin sushi rolls (hosomaki) or the thicker rolls (futomaki), such as California rolls. However, sushi rice can also be a flavour-packed side dish to all manner of Japanese-inspired grills and stir-fries. Try it with soy-marinated salmon, for example, or as the staple to soak up the juices from barbecued beef teriyaki.

pasta

It's hardly a coincidence that pasta features on so many people's desert island essential lists. Quick to prepare and with infinite possibilities for varying both the actual shapes and the accompaniments, pasta is the busy cook's best friend. It's also deeply comforting – so if you ever should find yourself castaway, or just stuck for inspiration for what to cook, these recipes will come to the rescue.

roasted eggplant and chilli pasta

chunky pesto pasta

lemon and garlic prawn pasta

roasted eggplant and chilli pasta

300g (10½ oz) baby eggplants (aubergines), halved
⅓ cup (80ml/2½ fl oz) olive oil
1 long red chilli, halved
sea salt and cracked black pepper
2 tablespoons olive oil, extra
3 cloves garlic, sliced
2 cups (500ml/16 fl oz) tomato puree
¼ cup oregano leaves
400g (14 oz) orecchiette pasta
250g (8 fl oz) fresh ricotta cheese

Preheat the oven to 200°C (400°F). Place the eggplant, oil, chilli, salt and pepper in a baking dish and toss to coat. Roast the eggplant mixture for 15–20 minutes or until browned. Chop the roasted chilli and set the mixture aside. Heat a medium saucepan over medium heat. Add the extra oil and garlic and cook for 1–2 minutes. Add the tomato puree, bring to the boil and simmer for 5 minutes. Stir through the oregano. Cook the pasta in a large saucepan of salted boiling water for 10–12 minutes or until al dente. Drain and return to the pan. Add the eggplant and chilli mixture, the tomato sauce and ricotta and toss to combine. Serves 4.

chunky pesto pasta

½ cup pine nuts
2 cloves garlic
½ cup (125ml/4 fl oz) olive oil
1½ cups basil leaves
400g (14 oz) penne pasta
sea salt and cracked black pepper
1 cup finely grated parmesan cheese

Preheat the oven to 180°C (350°F). Place the pine nuts on a baking tray and roast for 3 minutes or until golden. Allow to cool. Place the pine nuts, garlic and oil in a food processor and process in short bursts until roughly chopped. Add the basil and process until just combined. Set the pesto aside. Cook the pasta in a saucepan of salted boiling water for 10–12 minutes or until al dente. Drain and return to the pan. Stir through the pesto, salt, pepper and parmesan. Serves 4.

lemon and garlic prawn pasta

400g (14 oz) angel hair pasta
50g (1¾ oz) unsalted butter
2 cloves garlic, crushed
400g (14 oz) green (raw) prawns (shrimp), peeled with tails intact
sea salt and cracked black pepper
1 cup (250ml/8 fl oz) store-bought fish stock
2 tablespoons lemon zest
2 tablespoons lemon juice
½ cup chopped green onions (scallions)
1 cup basil leaves
shaved parmesan cheese, to serve

Cook the pasta in a large saucepan of salted boiling water for 2–3 minutes or until al dente. Drain and return to the pan. Heat a non-stick frying pan over high heat. Add the butter, garlic, prawns, salt and pepper and cook for 1 minute. Add the stock and cook for a further 2 minutes or until the prawns are cooked through. Add the prawn mixture to the pasta with the lemon zest and juice, green onions and basil and toss to coat. Top with the parmesan. Serves 4.

cheese and caramelised beetroot pasta

2 x 400g (14 oz) bunches baby beetroot, trimmed and halved
5 cloves garlic
½ cup sage leaves
1 tablespoon brown sugar
¼ cup (60ml/2 fl oz) olive oil
400g (14 oz) farfalle (butterfly) pasta
1 cup finely grated parmesan cheese
1 cup (250g/8 oz) mascarpone cheese
125g (4 oz) goat's curd

Preheat the oven to 180°C (350°F). Place the beetroot, garlic, sage, sugar and oil in a baking dish and toss to coat. Roast the mixture for 30–35 minutes or until the beetroot is tender. Peel the garlic and mash to a paste. Set aside and keep warm. Cook the pasta in a large saucepan of salted boiling water for 10–12 minutes or until al dente. Drain and return to the pan. Stir through the parmesan, mascarpone, beetroot mixture and garlic, top with the goat's curd. Serves 4.

cheese and caramelised beetroot pasta

white bean, rosemary and pancetta spaghetti   chorizo and tomato pasta

crispy sage and brown butter pasta

white bean, rosemary and pancetta spaghetti

400g (14 oz) spaghetti
2 tablespoons olive oil
10 slices pancetta, chopped
3 teaspoons rosemary leaves
400g (14 oz) can white (cannellini) beans, drained and rinsed
1 teaspoon finely grated lemon rind
2 tablespoons lemon juice
sea salt and cracked black pepper

Cook the pasta in a large saucepan of salted boiling water for
10–12 minutes or until al dente. Drain and return to the pan.
Meanwhile, heat a non-stick frying pan over high heat. Add the
oil and pancetta and cook for 4 minutes or until crisp. Add the
rosemary, white beans and lemon rind and cook for 3 minutes
or until heated through. Toss the bean mixture, lemon juice,
salt and pepper through the pasta. Serves 4.

chorizo and tomato pasta

400g (14 oz) rigatoni pasta
4 x 100g (3½ oz) chorizo or other dry, spicy sausages, thinly sliced
1 red capsicum (bell pepper), cut into 2cm (1 in) pieces
2 cups (500ml/16 fl oz) tomato puree
½ cup (125ml/4 fl oz) white wine
2 teaspoons sugar
½ cup black olives
2 tablespoons chopped flat-leaf parsley leaves
cracked black pepper
finely grated parmesan cheese, to serve

Cook the pasta in a large saucepan of salted boiling water for
10–12 minutes or until al dente. Drain and return to the saucepan
to keep warm. While the pasta is cooking, heat a non-stick frying
pan over medium heat and cook the sausage and capsicum for
4 minutes or until the sausage is browned and crisp. Add the tomato
puree, wine, sugar, olives, parsley and pepper. Cook for 5 minutes
until slightly reduced, spoon the tomato sauce over the pasta and
serve with the parmesan. Serves 4.

crispy sage and brown butter pasta

400g (14 oz) spaghetti
100g (3½ oz) unsalted butter
⅔ cup sage leaves
2 tablespoons lemon juice
sea salt and cracked black pepper
shaved parmesan cheese, to serve

Cook the pasta in a large saucepan of salted boiling water for
10–12 minutes or until al dente. Drain and set aside. Heat a large
non-stick frying pan over medium heat. Add the butter and stir until
melted. Add the sage and cook for 2–3 minutes or until the sage is
crispy and the butter is browned. Stir through the lemon juice, pasta,
salt and pepper and toss to combine. Top with the parmesan to serve.
Serves 4.

veal pasta ragout

400g (14 oz) pappardelle or lasagne pasta sheets
1 quantity veal ragout (recipe, page 91)
shaved parmesan cheese, to serve

Cook the pasta in a large saucepan of salted boiling water for
10–12 minutes or until al dente. Drain and divide the pasta among
serving bowls. Top with the veal ragout and shaved parmesan to
serve. Serves 6.

veal pasta ragout

mushroom and thyme creamy pasta

spinach and ricotta baked pasta

chicken spaghetti salad

mushroom and thyme creamy pasta

400g (14 oz) tagliatelle pasta
1 tablespoon olive oil
50g (1¾ oz) unsalted butter
3 eschalots, chopped
200g (7 oz) oyster mushrooms
200g (7 oz) button mushrooms, halved
200g (7 oz) Swiss brown mushrooms, halved
1 tablespoon thyme leaves
1 cup (250ml/8 fl oz) (single or pouring) cream
½ cup (125ml/4 fl oz) chicken stock
finely grated parmesan cheese, to serve

Cook the pasta in a large saucepan of salted boiling water for 10–12 minutes or until al dente. Drain and keep warm. Heat a large non-stick frying pan over medium heat. Add the oil, butter and eschalots and cook for 2–3 minutes or until soft. Add the mushrooms and thyme and cook for 5–6 minutes. Stir in the cream and stock and simmer for a further 5 minutes or until the mushrooms are tender. Add the pasta and toss to combine. Top with the parmesan. Serves 4.

spinach and ricotta baked pasta

500g (1 lb) rigatoni pasta
2 x 500g (1 lb) bunches English spinach, stems removed
750g (1½ lb) fresh ricotta cheese
300ml (10½ fl oz) sour cream
4 eggs, lightly beaten
1 cup grated parmesan cheese
2 tablespoons chopped dill
sea salt and cracked black pepper

Preheat the oven to 180°C (350°F). Cook the pasta in a large saucepan of salted boiling water for 10–12 minutes or until al dente. Drain. Place the pasta in a greased 16-cup (4 litre/128 fl oz) capacity baking dish. Blanch the spinach in a saucepan of boiling water, drain and squeeze to remove liquid. Roughly chop the spinach and place in a bowl. Mix in the ricotta, sour cream, eggs, parmesan, dill, salt and pepper. Spoon the mixture over the pasta. Bake for 25–30 minutes or until golden. Stand for 5 minutes before cutting. Serves 6.

chicken spaghetti salad

400g (14 oz) spaghetti
2 teaspoons olive oil
3 x 200g (7 oz) chicken breast fillets
100g (3½ oz) baby spinach leaves, roughly shredded
250g (8 oz) cherry tomatoes, quartered
sea salt and cracked black pepper
1 quantity mustard dressing (recipe, page 90)

Cook the pasta in a large saucepan of salted boiling water for 10–12 minutes or until al dente. Drain. Heat a large frying pan over medium heat, add the oil and chicken and cook until golden and cooked through. Cool slightly then shred. Combine the chicken with the spinach leaves, tomatoes, salt, pepper and pasta. Toss through the mustard dressing. Serves 4.

pasta with prosciutto, ricotta and peas

400g (14 oz) linguine pasta
8 slices prosciutto, sliced
6 green onions (scallions), sliced
1½ cups frozen peas
1 cup (250ml/8 fl oz) chicken stock
⅓ cup shredded mint leaves
sea salt and cracked black pepper
200g (7 oz) fresh ricotta cheese

Cook the pasta in a large saucepan of salted boiling water for 10–12 minutes or until al dente. Drain and return to the saucepan to keep warm. Cook the prosciutto in a non-stick frying pan over medium heat until crisp and browned. Remove and set aside. Add the green onions, peas and stock to the pan and simmer for 2–3 minutes or until slightly reduced. Set one half of the pea mixture aside and roughly mash the other half. To serve, toss the mashed and whole pea mixtures with the prosciutto, mint, pasta, salt and pepper. Crumble the ricotta over the top. Serves 4.

pasta with prosciutto, ricotta and peas

winter greens and pancetta fettuccine

smoked trout, caper and ricotta spaghetti

pumpkin and sage brown butter pasta

winter greens and pancetta fettuccine

400g (14 oz) fettuccine pasta
30g (1 oz) butter
1 teaspoon olive oil
1 garlic clove, crushed
1 brown onion, chopped
1 tablespoon thyme leaves
1 bunch silver beet (Swiss chard), trimmed and chopped
½ cup (125 ml/4 fl oz) chicken stock
2 tablespoons finely grated lemon rind
sea salt and cracked black pepper
12 slices pancetta, grilled (broiled)
finely grated parmesan cheese, to serve

Cook the pasta in a large saucepan of salted boiling water for 10–12 minutes or until al dente. Drain and keep warm. Heat a large non-stick frying pan over high heat. Add the butter, oil, garlic, onion and thyme and cook for 2 minutes. Add the silver beet and toss for 1 minute or until just starting to wilt. Pour in the stock, cover and cook for 4–5 minutes or until the silver beet is wilted and cooked through. Stir in the lemon rind, salt and pepper. Add the silver beet mixture to the pasta and toss to combine. To serve, top with the pancetta and parmesan. Serves 4.

smoked trout, caper and ricotta spaghetti

400g (14 oz) spaghetti
1 quantity lemon caper salsa (recipe, page 89)
½ cup finely grated parmesan cheese
cracked black pepper
200g (7 oz) smoked trout slices
70g (2½ oz) baby spinach leaves
150g (5¼ oz) ricotta cheese
shaved parmesan cheese, to serve

Cook the pasta in a large saucepan of salted boiling water for 10–12 minutes or until al dente. Drain and return to the pan. Add the lemon caper salsa to the pasta with the parmesan and pepper and toss gently to combine. Divide the trout slices among four plates. Top with the pasta, spinach, ricotta and shaved parmesan. Serves 4.

pumpkin and sage brown butter pasta

1kg (2¼ lb) pumpkin, peeled and diced
olive oil
400g (14 oz) pappardelle or fettuccine pasta
75g (2½ oz) butter
3 tablespoons whole sage leaves
1 cup finely grated parmesan cheese
sea salt and cracked black pepper

Preheat the oven to 190°C (375°F). Place the pumpkin in a baking dish and sprinkle with a little olive oil. Bake for 30 minutes or until golden and soft. Just before the pumpkin is ready, cook the pasta in a large saucepan of lightly salted boiling water until al dente. Drain. While the pasta is cooking, place the butter and sage in a saucepan over low to medium heat and allow the butter to simmer until a golden brown colour. To serve, place the pasta in serving plates and top with the pumpkin and parmesan. Spoon over the brown butter and sage leaves and season with salt and pepper. Serves 4.

vongole pasta

400g (14 oz) linguine pasta
1kg (2¼ lb) vongole (clams), cleaned
1 quantity chilli tomato sauce (recipe, page 88)

Cook the pasta in a large saucepan of salted boiling water for 10–12 minutes or until al dente. Drain and keep warm. Heat a large, deep frying pan with 1cm (½ in) water to simmering and add the vongole. Cover and cook for 3 minutes or until all the shells have opened. Drain, reserving the cooking liquid, and discard any unopened vongole. Place the chilli tomato sauce in a large saucepan over medium heat. Add the vongole cooking liquid and simmer for a further 3 minutes. Toss the vongole with the sauce and serve on top of the pasta. Serves 4.

vongole pasta

spaghetti with tomatoes and capers

pasta with buttered broccoli

fettuccine carbonara

spaghetti with tomatoes and capers

400g (14 oz) spaghetti

2 tablespoons olive oil

250g punnet cherry truss tomatoes

¼ cup salted capers, rinsed and drained

2 cloves garlic, chopped

2 long red chillies, seeded and sliced

2 teaspoons lemon zest

¼ cup (60ml/2 fl oz) lemon juice

2 cups baby rocket (arugula) leaves

½ cup finely grated parmesan cheese

Cook the pasta in a large saucepan of salted boiling water for 10–12 minutes or until al dente. Drain and keep warm. Heat the oil in a non-stick frying pan over medium heat. Add the tomatoes and cook for 5–8 minutes, then add the capers and garlic and cook for a further 1 minute. Add the chilli, lemon zest and juice and cook for another 1 minute. Toss the tomato mixture with the rocket, parmesan and pasta and serve immediately. Serves 4.

pasta with buttered broccoli

1kg (2¼ lb) broccoli, cut into small florets

400g (14 oz) orecchiette or penne pasta

1 tablespoon olive oil

2 tablespoons butter

2 cloves garlic, sliced

2 small red chillies, seeded and chopped

1 tablespoon lemon zest

sea salt and cracked black pepper

finely grated parmesan cheese, to serve

Steam the broccoli over boiling water for 4 minutes or until tender. Set aside. Cook the pasta in a large saucepan of salted boiling water for 10–12 minutes or until al dente. Drain. While the pasta is cooking, heat a non-stick frying pan over medium heat. Add the oil, butter, garlic, chillies and lemon zest and cook for 2 minutes. Add the broccoli, toss to combine and heat through. Toss the broccoli mixture with the pasta, salt and pepper. Divide among serving plates and serve with parmesan. Serves 4.

fettuccine carbonara

400g (14 oz) fettuccine or pappardelle pasta

6 rashers bacon or 300g (10½ oz) leg ham, cut into thin strips

3 green onions (scallions), sliced

4 egg yolks

½ cup (125ml/4 fl oz) (single or pouring) cream

½ cup finely grated parmesan cheese

2 tablespoons chopped flat-leaf parsley leaves

grated parmesan cheese, extra, to serve

Cook the pasta in a large saucepan of salted boiling water for 10–12 minutes or until al dente. Drain and keep hot. While the pasta is cooking, heat a non-stick frying pan over medium heat. Cook the bacon and onions for 3–4 minutes or until the bacon is crisp. Whisk the egg yolks with the cream and parmesan in a bowl and toss through the hot pasta, coating it well. Stir in the bacon mixture and parsley and top with the extra parmesan. Serves 4.

pea, fennel and mint spaghetti

400g (14 oz) spaghetti

1 tablespoon olive oil

1 onion, finely chopped

½ cup (125ml/4 fl oz) chicken stock

⅓ cup (80ml/2½ fl oz) (single or pouring) cream

3 cups frozen peas, defrosted

⅓ cup mint leaves, torn

¼ cup (60ml/2 fl oz) lemon juice

⅔ cup grated parmesan cheese

2 bulbs baby fennel, finely sliced

shaved parmesan cheese, to serve

Cook the pasta in a large saucepan of salted boiling water for 10–12 minutes or until al dente. Drain and return to the pan. While the pasta is cooking, heat a medium saucepan over medium–high heat. Add the oil and onion and cook for 3 minutes until softened. Add the stock, cream and peas, cover and simmer for 2 minutes or until the peas are tender. Mash or process half the pea mixture to a coarse consistency. Toss both the pea mixtures, mint, lemon juice, parmesan and fennel through the pasta, top with the shaved parmesan. Serves 4.

pea, fennel and mint spaghetti

spaghetti and meatballs

250g (8 oz) beef mince
250g (8 oz) pork mince
2 cloves garlic, chopped
1 egg
2 tablespoons finely grated parmesan cheese
½ cup (25g/⅞ oz) fresh breadcrumbs
¼ cup chopped flat-leaf parsley leaves
sea salt and cracked black pepper
400g (14 oz) spaghetti
2 teaspoons olive oil
1 quantity basic tomato sauce (recipe, page 88)
⅓ cup (80ml/2½ fl oz) beef stock
¼ cup (60ml/2 fl oz) red wine

Combine the beef and pork mince, garlic, egg, parmesan, breadcrumbs, parsley, salt and pepper in a large bowl. Shape spoonfuls of the mixture into walnut-sized balls. Place on a tray lined with non-stick baking paper. Refrigerate for 15 minutes. Cook the pasta in a large saucepan of salted boiling water for 10–12 minutes or until al dente. Drain and keep warm. Meanwhile, heat the oil in a large non-stick frying pan over medium heat. Cook the meatballs for 4–5 minutes, or until browned and cooked through. Drain on absorbent paper.

Heat the basic tomato sauce, stock and wine in a large saucepan over medium heat and simmer for 4 minutes. Toss the meatballs through the sauce and place on top of the pasta in bowls. Serves 4.

lasagne

500g (1 lb) fresh lasagne pasta sheets
1 quantity bolognese sauce (recipe, page 88)
¾ cup grated mozzarella cheese
white sauce
80g (2½ oz) butter
⅓ cup (50g/1¾ oz) plain (all-purpose) flour
4 cups (1 litre/32 fl oz) milk
¾ cup grated parmesan cheese
sea salt and cracked black pepper

To make the white sauce, place the butter in a saucepan over medium heat and allow to melt. Add the flour and stir to a smooth paste. Whisk in the milk and then stir until the sauce has boiled and thickened. Stir in the parmesan and add the salt and pepper. Set aside to cool to room temperature.

Preheat the oven to 190°C (375°F). Grease a 20cm (8 in) square ovenproof dish and line with lasagne sheets. Thinly spread over a quarter of the bolognese sauce, then spoon over a quarter of the white sauce and cover with more lasagne sheets. Repeat the layers, finishing with white sauce. Sprinkle with the mozzarella and bake for 25–30 minutes or until golden brown and cooked through. Serves 4.

spaghetti and meatballs

lasagne

rice

Rice enjoys such status in Asia that most countries have a universal greeting that loosely translates as 'have you eaten rice yet?' Indeed rice is such an adaptable ingredient that it's little wonder it's earning similar eminence in the West. Far from being relegated to the side of the plate, these days rice has evolved as the main event in easy bakes, stir-fries, paella, risottos, rice cakes and salads.

Thai fried rice

pancetta and sweet potato baked risotto

parmesan risotto balls

Thai fried rice

2 tablespoons vegetable oil

2 eggs, lightly beaten

2 teaspoons grated ginger

2 garlic cloves, crushed

16 green (raw) prawns (shrimp), peeled, tails intact

2 cups cooked long-grain rice

1 cup frozen peas

275g (9½ oz) bunch baby bok choy, trimmed and quartered

1 tablespoon soy sauce

2 teaspoons lime juice

1 cup coriander (cilantro) leaves, to serve

Heat 2 teaspoons of the oil in a large wok over high heat. Add the eggs and cook for 1 minute. Remove the omelette from the wok and roughly chop. Add the remaining oil, ginger, garlic and prawns and cook for 2–3 minutes or until the prawns are cooked through. Add the rice, peas, bok choy, soy and lime juice and stir-fry for a further 2 minutes or until the bok choy is tender. Add the omelette and toss to combine. Divide the fried rice among bowls and top with the coriander to serve. Serves 4.

pancetta and sweet potato baked risotto

1½ cups arborio or carnaroli rice

4½ cups (1.25 litres/36 fl oz) chicken stock

1 cup finely grated parmesan cheese

sea salt and cracked black pepper

400g (14 oz) sweet potato (kumara), roasted until soft

4 slices pancetta, cooked to crispy

¼ cup torn sage leaves, fried to crispy

melted unsalted butter, for drizzling

Preheat the oven to 180°C (350°F). Place the rice and stock in a 10-cup (2.5 litre/80 fl oz) capacity ceramic ovenproof dish and stir to combine. Cover tightly with aluminium (aluminum) foil and bake for 40 minutes or until most of the stock is absorbed and the rice is al dente. Add the parmesan, salt, pepper, sweet potato and pancetta and stir to combine. To serve, top with the sage and drizzle with butter. Serves 4.

parmesan risotto balls

1 teaspoon thyme leaves

1 quantity basic risotto (recipe, page 19), cooled

125g (4 oz) block parmesan cheese

vegetable oil, for deep-frying

Mix the thyme into the basic risotto. Divide the risotto into 10 portions and shape each portion to a ball. Cut the parmesan into 10 pieces. Place a piece of parmesan in the middle of each ball and press the risotto over to enclose it. Heat the oil in a saucepan over medium heat. Deep-fry the balls, in batches, for 3–4 minutes, or until golden. Drain on absorbent paper. Makes 10.

vegetable and egg fried rice

1½ tablespoons vegetable oil

4 eggs, lightly beaten

1 teaspoon sesame oil

4 cups cooked jasmine rice

200g (7 oz) snake beans, chopped and blanched

1 cup frozen peas, defrosted

4 green onions (scallions), sliced

soy sauce, to serve

Heat two teaspoons of the vegetable oil in a wok or a large non-stick frying pan over high heat. Add the egg and swirl around the wok or pan. Cook for 1 minute, turn the omelette out onto a board, roll up and slice. Add the remaining vegetable oil, sesame oil and rice to the wok and stir-fry for 2–3 minutes. Add the beans and peas and stir-fry for a further 2–3 minutes or until the peas are tender. Spoon into bowls, top with the green onion and egg and sprinkle with the soy to serve. Serves 4.

+ Chopped and fried Chinese sausage, chicken, pork or duck can be added to this recipe.

vegetable and egg fried rice

simple eggcup sushi   baked risotto with pumpkin and fetta

five-spice pork fried rice

simple eggcup sushi

1 quantity sushi rice (recipe, page 21)
600g (1¼ lb) smoked salmon slices
soy sauce, to serve

Line an eggcup with plastic wrap. Place a slice of salmon around the inside of the eggcup. Press the sushi rice firmly into the eggcup, ensuring that the rice comes right to the top. Turn the sushi out onto a serving platter. Repeat with the remaining sushi rice and salmon. Serve with the soy. Makes 16.

baked risotto with pumpkin and fetta

1 tablespoon olive oil
300g (10½ oz) peeled and chopped pumpkin
2 leeks, sliced
1 tablespoon thyme leaves
2 cups arborio or carnaroli rice
5 cups (1.25 litres/40 fl oz) chicken or vegetable stock
1 cup frozen green peas
¾ cup grated parmesan cheese
2 tablespoons basil leaves
sea salt and cracked black pepper
100g (3½ oz) fetta cheese

Preheat the oven to 200°C (400°F). Heat a non-stick frying pan over high heat. Add the oil, pumpkin, leek and thyme and cook for 5 minutes or until the leek is lightly browned. Spoon the vegetable mixture into a 10-cup (2.5 litre/80 fl oz) capacity ceramic ovenproof dish. Add the rice and stock and stir. Cover tightly with aluminium (aluminum) foil and bake for 30 minutes. Add the peas, re-cover and cook for a further 10 minutes. Remove the risotto from the oven, add the parmesan, basil, salt and pepper and stir for 4 minutes or until the risotto has thickened. To serve, divide among bowls and crumble over the fetta. Serves 4.

five-spice pork fried rice

2 teaspoons vegetable oil
1 teaspoon Chinese five-spice powder
1 tablespoon grated ginger
½ teaspoon chilli flakes
2 x 250g (8 oz) pork fillets, thinly sliced
2 tablespoons vegetable oil, extra
6 cups cooked rice
4 green onions (scallions), sliced
200g (7 oz) snow peas (mange tout), sliced lengthways
2 tablespoons soy sauce
hoisin sauce, to serve

Heat a non-stick frying pan over high heat. Add the oil, five-spice, ginger and chilli and cook for 30 seconds. Add the pork and cook for 5 minutes or until well browned. Remove from the pan and set aside. Add the extra oil and rice and cook, stirring, for 5 minutes or until the rice is heated through. Add the green onion and snow peas and cook for 2 minutes. Stir through the cooked pork and soy sauce. Divide among bowls and serve with the hoisin, if desired. Serves 4.

soy chicken and rice pot

½ cup (125ml/4 fl oz) soy sauce
⅔ cup (165ml/5 fl oz) sherry or Chinese cooking wine
⅓ cup (75g/2⅔ oz) sugar
1 tablespoon grated ginger
4 x 200g (7 oz) chicken breast fillets
2 cups jasmine rice
3½ cups (875ml/28 fl oz) water

Place the soy, sherry, sugar and ginger in a non-stick frying pan over high heat and bring to the boil. Add the chicken fillets and cook for 2 minutes each side. Place the rice and water into a deep frying pan over high heat. Cook, uncovered, for 4–5 minutes, or until tunnels have formed in the rice and most of the water has been absorbed. Top with the chicken, cover and cook over low heat for 5–6 minutes or until the chicken is cooked through. While the chicken is cooking, simmer the soy mixture for 2 minutes or until syrupy. To serve, divide the chicken and rice among plates and top with the soy mixture. Serves 4.

soy chicken and rice pot

baked pea and pancetta risotto

brown rice and herb salad

crispy rice omelette

baked pea and pancetta risotto

40g (1½ oz) butter
1 onion, chopped
2 cloves garlic, crushed
3 teaspoons finely grated lemon rind
2 cups arborio or carnaroli rice
6 cups (1.5 litres/48 fl oz) chicken stock
2 cups (250g/8 oz) fresh or frozen peas
1 tablespoon chopped dill leaves
1 tablespoon chopped flat-leaf parsley leaves
⅓ cup finely grated parmesan cheese
sea salt and cracked black pepper
8 slices pancetta, grilled (broiled)

Preheat the oven to 200°C (400°F). Heat the butter in a non-stick
frying pan over medium heat. Add the onion, garlic and lemon rind
and cook for 4 minutes or until the onion is softened. Place the mixture
in a 10-cup (2.5 litre/80 fl oz) ceramic ovenproof dish and add the rice
and stock. Cover tightly with a lid or aluminium (aluminum) foil and
bake for 35 minutes. Stir through the peas, dill and parsley and return
to the oven for 5 minutes. Remove the risotto from the oven and stir
for 3–4 minutes or until thickened. Fold through the parmesan, salt
and pepper and serve with the grilled pancetta. Serves 4.

brown rice and herb salad

2 cups cooked brown rice, cooled
2 cups baby rocket (arugula) leaves
½ cup mint leaves
½ cup flat-leaf parsley leaves
3 green onions (scallions), sliced
1 tomato, chopped
⅓ cup roasted pine nuts
sea salt and cracked black pepper
¼ cup (60ml/2 fl oz) lemon juice
2 tablespoons olive oil

Place the rice, rocket, mint, parsley, green onion, tomato, pine nuts,
salt, pepper, lemon juice and olive oil in a large bowl and toss to
combine. Serves 4.

crispy rice omelette

2 tablespoons peanut oil
1½ cups cooked jasmine or short-grain rice
4 green onions (scallions), sliced thinly
2 small red chillies, seeded and chopped
150g (5¼ oz) snow peas (mange tout), sliced lengthways
6 eggs, lightly beaten

Preheat the oven to 180°C (350°F). Heat a 20cm (8 in) non-stick,
ovenproof frying pan over high heat. Add the oil and rice and cook,
stirring, for 5 minutes or until the rice is slightly crisp. Add the green
onions, chillies and snow peas and cook for 2 minutes. Pour the eggs
over and stir for 1 minute. Reduce the heat to low and cook, without
stirring, for 5 minutes. Finish cooking the omelette in the oven for
3 minutes or until the omelette has set. Cut into slices. Serves 4.

prawn paella

6 cups (1.5 litres/48 fl oz) chicken stock
2 tablespoons olive oil
1 onion, chopped
2 cloves garlic, crushed
2 small red chillies, finely sliced
2 x 100g (3½ oz) chorizo sausages, sliced
2 cups arborio rice
2 cups chopped tomatoes
2 tablespoons tomato paste
1 cup (250ml/8 fl oz) dry white wine
18 green (raw) prawns (shrimp), unpeeled
¼ cup chopped flat-leaf parsley leaves
lemon wedges, to serve

Place the stock in a saucepan over medium heat and bring to a simmer.
Heat a large saucepan or paella pan over medium heat. Add the oil,
onion, garlic, chilli and chorizo and cook for 5–7 minutes or until the
onions are soft and the chorizo is golden. Stir in the rice, tomatoes,
tomato paste and wine and cook for 2–3 minutes. Add cups of the hot
stock to the rice, stirring continuously, until each cup is absorbed and
the rice is al dente. Add the prawns and cook for 2–3 minutes or until
cooked through. Add the parsley and serve with lemon. Serves 6.

prawn paella

lettuce-cup sushi

lime and coconut chicken rice

nut-spiced pilaf and cumin lamb

lettuce-cup sushi

2 baby cos (romaine) lettuces, outer leaves discarded
1 quantity sushi rice (recipe, page 21)
wasabi paste (see glossary), to serve
16 sprigs baby watercress or mustard cress
200g (7 oz) sashimi grade tuna, sliced
2 sheets nori (see glossary), cut into strips

Separate the young leaves from the lettuce, wash and dry. Spoon 1–2 teaspoons sushi rice into the lettuce cups. Place a little wasabi on the rice, then top with a sprig of watercress, a slice of tuna and a strip of the nori. Makes 16.

lime and coconut chicken rice

2 cups jasmine rice
2½ cups (625ml/20 fl oz) water
3 cups shredded cooked chicken
1 baby cos (romaine) lettuce, trimmed, leaves separated
creamy coconut dressing
¾ cup (185ml/6 fl oz) coconut cream
¾ cup (185ml/6 fl oz) lime juice
¼ cup (60ml/2 fl oz) fish sauce
½ cup chopped mint leaves
1 long red chilli, seeded and chopped

To make the dressing, combine the coconut cream, lime juice, fish sauce, mint and chilli in a small bowl or jar.

Place the rice and water in a saucepan over medium heat and cook, uncovered, until most of the liquid has been absorbed and tunnels have formed in the rice. Cover and set aside for 5 minutes. When the rice is cooked, toss with the dressing and chicken and place in a serving bowl lined with the cos leaves. Serves 4.

nut-spiced pilaf and cumin lamb

1½ cups basmati rice
1 x 100g (3½ oz) brown onion, finely chopped
1 cinnamon stick
2 bay leaves
2 cardamom pods, bruised
2½ cups (625ml/20 fl oz) chicken stock
2 teaspoons ground coriander (cilantro)
2 teaspoons ground cumin
¼ teaspoon chilli powder
1 teaspoon sea salt
4 x 200g (7 oz) lamb backstraps (boneless loin), trimmed
1 tablespoon olive oil
¼ cup roasted slivered almonds
½ cup chopped flat-leaf parsley leaves

Place the rice, onion, cinnamon, bay leaves, cardamom and stock in a medium saucepan over medium heat and bring to the boil. Cook for 5–8 minutes or until most of the stock has been absorbed. Turn off the heat and rest for 10–12 minutes or until the rice is tender. Set aside and keep warm. Combine the coriander, cumin, chilli and salt, then rub the mixture on the lamb. Heat the oil in a large non-stick frying pan over high heat. Cook the lamb for 3–4 minutes each side for medium or until cooked to your liking. Stir the almonds and parsley through the pilaf. Slice the lamb and serve with the pilaf. Serves 4.

cut-out sushi

1 quantity sushi rice (recipe, page 21)
1 sheet nori (see glossary)
wasabi paste (see glossary), to serve
1 Lebanese cucumber, thinly sliced
200g (7 oz) smoked salmon or smoked trout slices
18 sprigs baby watercress or mustard cress

Press the sushi rice into a lightly greased 16 x 25cm (6 x 10 in) tin. Cover and place in the fridge to chill. Use a greased 4½cm (1¾ in) cookie cutter to cut out 18 rounds of nori and set aside, then cut out 18 rounds of rice. Place the rice on top of the nori, top with a little of the wasabi, cucumber, salmon and watercress. Makes 18.

cut-out sushi

mixed mushroom risotto

10g (⅓ oz) dried porcini mushrooms

1½ cups (375ml/12 fl oz) boiling water

4 cups (1 litre/32 fl oz) beef or vegetable stock

½ cup (125ml/4 fl oz) red wine

1½ tablespoons olive oil

20g (¾ oz) butter

1 leek, trimmed and sliced

2 cloves garlic, chopped

2 cups arborio or other risotto rice

550g (1⅛ lb) mixed mushrooms (portobello, Swiss brown, shiitake)

sea salt and cracked black pepper

1 tablespoon chopped flat-leaf parsley leaves

Soak the porcini mushrooms in the boiling water for 15 minutes. Strain, reserving the liquid, and finely slice the mushrooms. Bring the stock, wine and porcini liquid to a slow simmer. Meanwhile, cook 1 tablespoon of the oil, butter, leek and garlic in a large saucepan over medium heat for 6 minutes, or until the onion has softened. Add the rice, stirring to coat. When the rice is translucent, add the stock, 1 cup (250ml/8 fl oz) at a time, stirring continuously until each cup is absorbed and the rice is al dente (around 25–30 minutes). Cut any of the larger fresh mushrooms in half or into thick slices. Cook with the remaining oil in a frying pan over medium heat for 4–5 minutes or until golden, then fold through the risotto with the porcini mushrooms, salt, pepper and parsley. Serve immediately. Serves 4.

lemon and herb chicken pilaf

2 teaspoons vegetable oil

1 onion, chopped

2 teaspoons oregano leaves

sea salt and cracked black pepper

1 cup basmati or long-grain rice

3 cups (750ml/24 fl oz) chicken stock

4 x 200g (7 oz) chicken breast fillets, cut into thirds

2 teaspoons vegetable oil, extra

¼ cup chopped flat-leaf parsley leaves

100g (3½ oz) baby spinach leaves

1 tablespoon lemon zest

Heat a saucepan over medium–high heat. Add the oil, onion, oregano, salt and pepper and cook for 3 minutes or until the onion is soft. Add the rice and stock, bring to the boil, reduce the heat, cover with a tight-fitting lid and cook for 12 minutes or until the rice is al dente. Meanwhile, heat a non-stick frying pan over high heat. Sprinkle the chicken with salt and pepper and add to the pan with the extra oil. Cook for 4 minutes each side or until the chicken is cooked through. To serve, stir the parsley, spinach and lemon zest through the rice and divide among serving plates. Top with the chicken. Serves 4.

mixed mushroom risotto

lemon and herb chicken pilaf

noodles

Noodles symbolise long life in many Asian cultures so they usually feature on birthday, New Year's and other celebration menus. However, as this collection of soups, salads and stir-fries shows, noodles' versatility, ease and speed of preparation make them stand-out stars of everyday as well as festive meals. Happy slurping.

lamb with black bean and garlic sauce

green tea soba noodles with vegetables

prawn noodle soup

lamb with black bean and garlic sauce

300g (10½ oz) dried rice stick noodles

2 x 200g (7 oz) lamb backstraps (boneless loins), trimmed

2 teaspoons vegetable oil

1 tablespoon store-bought black bean and garlic sauce

1⅓ cups (330ml/10½ fl oz) chicken stock

½ cup (125ml/4 fl oz) hoisin sauce

2 x 350g (12¼ oz) bunches gai larn (Chinese broccoli), trimmed

Place the noodles in a bowl and cover with boiling water for 10 minutes or until separated and tender. Drain and set aside. Place the lamb, oil and black bean sauce in a bowl and toss to coat. Heat a large non-stick frying pan over medium–high heat. Add the lamb and cook for 3 minutes each side or until cooked through. Remove the lamb from the pan, slice and keep warm. Add the stock and hoisin and cook for 1–2 minutes or until the sauce is thickened. Add the gai larn and noodles and cook for 2 minutes or until heated through. Divide the noodles between plates and top with the sliced lamb. Serves 4.

green tea soba noodles with vegetables

200g (7 oz) dried green tea soba noodles

2 teaspoons vegetable oil

2 cloves garlic, crushed

1 long red chilli, sliced

1 tablespoon finely grated ginger

200g (7 oz) shiitake or button mushrooms, sliced

1 x 275g (9½ oz) bunch baby bok choy, trimmed and quartered

1 cup (250ml/8 fl oz) chicken stock

⅓ cup (80ml/2½ fl oz) oyster sauce

600g (1¼ lb) firm tofu, chopped

4 green onions (scallions), sliced

Place the noodles in a medium saucepan of boiling water and cook for 5–6 minutes. Drain and set aside. Heat a large non-stick frying pan or wok over high heat. Add the oil, garlic, chilli and ginger and stir-fry for 1 minute. Stir in the mushrooms and cook for 2–3 minutes or until tender. Add the noodles, bok choy, stock and oyster sauce and cook for 1–2 minutes or until the bok choy is tender. Stir in the tofu, divide between bowls and top with the onion. Serves 4.

prawn noodle soup

8 cups (2 litres/64 fl oz) chicken stock

2 small red chillies, sliced

2 teaspoons sliced ginger

2 teaspoons soy sauce

2 tablespoons fish sauce

2 teaspoons brown sugar

300g (10½ oz) fresh thin egg noodles

160g (5½ oz) green beans, trimmed

300g (10½ oz) green (raw) prawns (shrimp), peeled with tails intact

4 green onions (scallions), sliced

Place the stock, chilli, ginger, soy, fish sauce and sugar in a medium saucepan over medium heat and bring to the boil. Add the noodles and cook for 1 minute. Stir in the beans and prawns and cook for 2–3 minutes or until the beans are tender and the prawns are cooked through. Divide the noodles between bowls, ladle over the soup and top with the prawns, beans and green onions to serve. Serves 4.

egg noodle soup with chilli pork

2 long red chillies, chopped

2 tablespoons chilli sauce

2 teaspoons soy sauce

2 x 250g (8 oz) pork fillets

8 cups (2 litres/64 fl oz) chicken stock

16 thin slices ginger

1½ tablespoons oyster sauce

2 x 350g (12¼ oz) bunches gai larn (Chinese broccoli), trimmed

400g (14 oz) fresh thin egg noodles

Combine the chilli, chilli sauce and soy in a bowl. Cut the pork fillet in half and coat in the chilli mixture. Preheat a medium non-stick frying pan over medium–low heat. Add the pork and cook, turning frequently, for 6 minutes. While the pork is cooking, place the stock, ginger and oyster sauce in a large saucepan and bring to the boil. Add the gai larn and cook for 3 minutes. Cook the noodles for 3 minutes in a saucepan of boiling water. Drain the noodles and place in bowls, top with the gai larn and pour the stock over. Arrange sliced pork on top. Serves 4.

egg noodle soup with chilli pork

Thai pork with noodles

barbecued duck with egg noodles

beef coconut noodles

Thai pork with noodles

750g (1½ lb) pork mince
1 stalk lemongrass, finely sliced
2 long red chillies, seeded and chopped
1 red onion, thinly sliced
150g (5¼ oz) dried bean thread noodles
¼ cup (60ml/2 fl oz) fish sauce
¼ cup (60ml/2 fl oz) lime juice
1½ tablespoons brown sugar
⅓ cup mint leaves

Heat a wok or non-stick frying pan over high heat. Add the mince and stir-fry for 5 minutes or until golden and cooked through. Place the mince in a bowl and mix with the lemongrass, chilli and onion. Break the noodles into short lengths and place in a heatproof bowl. Cover with boiling water and set aside for 5 minutes. Drain and set aside. Mix the fish sauce with the lime juice and sugar until well combined. Pour over the pork. Toss the pork mixture with the noodles and mint. Serves 4.

barbecued duck with egg noodles

375g (13¼ oz) fresh egg noodles
2 teaspoons sesame oil
1 tablespoon grated fresh ginger
¼ cup (60ml/2 fl oz) Chinese cooking wine or sherry
¼ cup (60ml/2 fl oz) hoisin sauce
¼ cup (60ml/2 fl oz) chicken stock
2 teaspoons sugar
1 Chinese barbecued duck (see glossary), chopped
350g (12¼ oz) bunch choy sum, trimmed and chopped
1 green onion (scallion), diagonally sliced

Cover the noodles with boiling water for 5 minutes. Drain and set aside. Heat a wok or non-stick frying pan over high heat. Add the sesame oil and ginger and stir-fry for 1 minute. Add the wine, hoisin, stock and sugar and cook for 3 minutes or until slightly reduced. Add the duck, noodles, choy sum and green onion and cook until heated through. Serves 4.

beef coconut noodles

2 x 200g (7 oz) beef fillet steaks, trimmed
olive oil, for brushing
sea salt and cracked black pepper
200g (7 oz) dried rice vermicelli noodles
2 tablespoons mint leaves
2 tablespoons basil leaves
1 long green chilli, thinly sliced
1 quantity coconut dressing (recipe, page 89)
flaked coconut, to serve

Brush the steaks with oil and sprinkle with salt and pepper. Heat a medium non-stick frying pan over high heat. Cook the steaks for 3–4 minutes each side or until cooked to your liking. Slice the steaks and set aside. Place the noodles in a bowl and cover with boiling water for 6–8 minutes, or until separated and tender. Drain, rinse with cold water and place in a bowl with the mint, basil, chilli and the beef slices. Toss to combine. Divide the noodle mixture among plates, spoon over the coconut dressing and top with the flaked coconut. Serves 4.

wasabi-crusted salmon with rice noodles

2 tablespoons vegetable oil
1 tablespoon wasabi paste (see glossary)
4 x 175g (6 oz) salmon fillets
300g (10½ oz) dried rice stick noodles
⅓ cup (80ml/2½ fl oz) soy sauce
⅔ cup (125g/4 oz) brown sugar
⅔ cup (165ml/5 fl oz) rice vinegar
1 small red chilli, chopped
½ cup mint leaves

Preheat the oven to 200°C (400°F). Combine the oil and wasabi and brush over the salmon. Place the salmon on a baking tray and cook for 10–12 minutes or until cooked to your liking. Allow to cool, then separate into pieces. Set aside. Place the noodles in a bowl, cover with boiling water for 10 minutes or until separated and tender. Drain. Place the soy, sugar and vinegar in a bowl and whisk together. Toss the soy mixture through the noodles with the chilli and mint. Divide the noodle mixture among bowls and top with the salmon. Serves 4.

wasabi-crusted salmon with rice noodles

vegetable laksa

bok choy and noodle stir-fry

spicy Thai chicken soup

vegetable laksa

1 tablespoon vegetable oil
¾ cup store-bought laksa paste
2 x 400ml (13 fl oz) cans coconut milk
2 cups (500ml/16 fl oz) water
1 kaffir lime leaf, thinly sliced
1 long red chilli, sliced
500g (1 lb) sweet potato (kumara), peeled and sliced
275g (9½ oz) bunch baby bok choy, trimmed and quartered
100g (3½ oz) snow peas (mange tout), trimmed and halved
150g (5¼ oz) dried rice vermicelli noodles, soaked and drained
1 cup bean sprouts
1 cup coriander (cilantro) leaves

Heat a wok or large non-stick frying pan over medium heat. Add the oil and laksa paste and cook for 1 minute. Add the coconut milk, water, lime leaf and chilli. Bring to the boil, add the sweet potato, reduce the heat to low and simmer for 15 minutes. Add the bok choy and snow peas and cook for 2 minutes or until the sweet potato is cooked and the bok choy is tender. Divide the noodles among bowls, spoon over the laksa broth and top with the sprouts and coriander to serve. Serves 4.

bok choy and noodle stir-fry

250g (8 oz) dried somen or Chinese wheat noodles
2 tablespoons peanut oil
2 tablespoons shredded ginger
2 cloves garlic, sliced
1 long red chilli, sliced
2 x 275g (9½ oz) bunches baby bok choy, trimmed and quartered
12 fresh shiitake or button mushrooms, halved
1 cup (250ml/8 fl oz) chicken or vegetable stock
2 tablespoons soy sauce

Place the noodles in a saucepan of boiling water, cook for 3 minutes or until soft. Drain. Heat the oil in a deep, non-stick frying pan or wok. Add the ginger, garlic and chilli and cook for 1 minute. Add the bok choy and mushrooms and cook for 2 minutes. Add the stock and soy and cook for 4 minutes or until the bok choy is soft. Divide the noodles among bowls and top with the bok choy mixture. Serves 4.

spicy Thai chicken soup

200g (7 oz) dried rice vermicelli noodles
1–2 tablespoons red or green curry paste
3 cups (750ml/24 fl oz) chicken stock
2 cups (500ml/16 fl oz) coconut cream
2 x 200g (7 oz) chicken breast fillets, sliced
150g (5¼ oz) green beans, halved

Soak the noodles in a bowl of boiling water for 6–8 minutes or until tender, then drain. Place the curry paste in a saucepan over medium–high heat and cook for 2 minutes. Add the chicken stock and coconut cream and simmer for 4 minutes. Add the chicken and beans and cook for 4 minutes. Add noodles and cook until heated through. To serve, divide among bowls. Serves 4.

Asian noodle soup with pork

375g (13¼ oz) dried rice stick noodles
6 cups (1.5 litres/48 fl oz) chicken stock
2 long red chillies, halved
2 slices ginger
2 garlic cloves, halved
⅓ cup (80ml/2½ fl oz) lime juice
2 teaspoons fish sauce
2 x 250g (8 oz) pork fillets, trimmed and sliced
2 x 275g (9½ oz) bunches baby bok choy, trimmed and quartered
1 long red chilli, extra, thinly sliced
bean sprouts, to serve
coriander (cilantro) leaves, to serve

Place the noodles in a bowl and cover with boiling water for 10 minutes or until separated and tender. Drain and set aside. Place the stock, chillies, ginger, garlic, lime juice and fish sauce in a large saucepan over medium heat. Bring the stock mixture to the boil and simmer for 5 minutes. Strain to remove the chilli, ginger and garlic and return the broth to the pan. Add the pork and simmer for 3 minutes or until the pork is cooked. Add the bok choy and noodles and cook for 1 minute or until the bok choy is tender. To serve, divide the noodle mixture among bowls and top with the chilli, bean sprouts and coriander. Serves 4.

Asian noodle soup with pork

lime beef and cucumber noodle salad   ginger pork noodle stir-fry

Thai lime and lemongrass chicken

lime beef and cucumber noodle salad

2 tablespoons peanut oil

750g (1½ lb) rump or topside steak, sliced

½ cup (125ml/4 fl oz) sweet chilli sauce

⅓ cup (80ml/2½ fl oz) lime juice

8 green onions (scallions), sliced

6 kaffir lime leaves, shredded

1 quantity cucumber noodle salad (recipe, page 89)

Heat the oil in a non-strick frying pan or wok over high heat. Add the beef and cook, in batches, for 5 minutes or until well sealed. Set aside. Add the chilli sauce, lime juice, green onions and lime leaves to the pan and cook for 4 minutes, then pour over the beef. Divide the noodle salad among serving plates. Top with the beef mixture. Serves 4.

ginger pork noodle stir-fry

1 tablespoon grated ginger

2 garlic cloves, crushed

2 tablespoons sweet chilli sauce

2 tablespoons kecap manis (see glossary)

2 x 250g (8 oz) pork fillets, trimmed and sliced

400g (14 oz) fresh udon noodles

1 tablespoon vegetable oil

1 red capsicum (bell pepper), sliced

2 green onions (scallions), sliced

1 x 350g (12¼ oz) bunch choy sum, trimmed

Combine the ginger, garlic, sweet chilli sauce and ketjap manis in a bowl. Add the pork and toss to coat. Place the noodles in a bowl and cover with boiling water. Stand for 5 minutes or until separated then drain. Heat the vegetable oil in a wok over high heat. Add the pork with the marinade and stir-fry for 3 minutes or until browned. Add the capsicum and stir-fry for 2 minutes. Add the onions, choy sum and noodles and stir-fry until the noodles are warmed. Serves 4.

Thai lime and lemongrass chicken

400g (14 oz) dried rice stick noodles

2 teaspoons vegetable oil

1 tablespoon grated ginger

1 stalk lemongrass, finely chopped

1 teaspoon chilli flakes

650g (1 lb 7 oz) chicken mince

¼ cup (60ml/2 fl oz) lime juice

¼ cup (60ml/2 fl oz) fish sauce

1 tablespoon sugar

¾ cup coriander (cilantro) leaves

¾ cup basil leaves

4 green onions (scallions), shredded

lime wedges, to serve

Place the noodles in a bowl and cover with boiling water for 10 minutes or until separated and tender. Drain. Heat a non-stick frying pan over high heat. Add the oil, ginger, lemongrass and chilli and cook for 1 minute. Add the mince and cook, stirring, for 6–7 minutes or until cooked through. Stir in the lime juice, fish sauce, sugar, coriander, basil and onions. Serve with hot noodles and lime wedges. Serves 4.

shredded duck and chilli noodle salad

150g (5¼ oz) dried bean thread noodles

4 long red chillies, seeded and sliced lengthways

4 long green chillies, seeded and sliced lengthways

⅓ cup chopped roasted peanuts

1½ cups coriander (cilantro) leaves

1½ cups Thai basil or basil leaves

1½ cups mint leaves

1 Chinese barbecued duck (see glossary), meat shredded

¼ cup (60ml/2 fl oz) lime juice

¼ cup (60ml/2 fl oz) fish sauce

2 tablespoons brown sugar

Place the noodles in a bowl and cover with boiling water. Allow to stand for 5 minutes or until soft. Drain. Toss the noodles with the chillies, peanuts, coriander, basil, mint and duck in a bowl. Combine the juice, fish sauce and sugar and pour over the noodles. Serves 4.

shredded duck and chilli noodle salad

noodle salad with crisp tofu

150g (5¼ oz) dried bean thread noodles
¼ cup (60ml/2 fl oz) peanut oil
375g (13¼ oz) firm tofu (see glossary), shredded
2 carrots, shredded
½ cup chopped roasted peanuts
½ cup coriander (cilantro) leaves
2 cucumbers, sliced lengthways
sesame dressing
1 tablespoon sesame oil
¼ cup (60ml/2 fl oz) soy sauce
1 tablespoon lemon juice

To make the dressing, combine the sesame oil, soy and lemon juice in a small jar or bowl and mix well.

Place the noodles in a bowl and cover with boiling water. Allow to stand for 5 minutes, then drain. Heat a non-stick frying pan over high heat. Add the oil and tofu and fry for 5 minutes or until crisp. Drain the tofu on absorbent paper. To serve, toss the noodles with the tofu, carrots, peanuts, coriander and dressing. Place the cucumber on serving plates and top with the salad. Serves 4.

combination rice noodles

400g (14 oz) dried rice stick noodles
2 tablespoons vegetable oil
2 teaspoons grated ginger
1 teaspoon chilli flakes
3 x 200g (7 oz) chicken breast fillets, sliced thinly
6 green onions (scallions), chopped
150g (5¼ oz) green beans, trimmed and halved
½ cup (125ml/4 fl oz) chicken stock
2 tablespoons lime juice
½ tablespoon brown sugar
1 tablespoon fish sauce
⅔ cup (165ml/5 fl oz) oyster sauce
½ cup coriander (cilantro) leaves
½ cup chopped roasted unsalted peanuts
3 eggs
1 teaspoon sesame oil

Place the noodles in a bowl and cover with boiling water for 10 minutes or until separated and tender. Drain and set aside. Heat a wok over high heat. Add the oil, ginger, chilli and chicken and stir-fry for 4 minutes or until the chicken is lightly browned. Add the onions and beans and cook for a further 3 minutes. Add the chicken stock, lime juice, sugar, fish sauce, oyster sauce and noodles and cook, stirring, for 2 minutes. Transfer the noodle mixture to a serving bowl and toss through the coriander and peanuts. Whisk together the eggs and sesame oil in a medium bowl, pour the egg mixture into the wok, swirl around and cook for 1 minute. Remove the omelette from the wok, slice and serve on top of the noodles. Serves 4.

noodle salad with crisp tofu

combination rice noodles

glossary, index

+ conversions

Asian greens

These leafy green vegetables from the brassica family are now becoming widely available. We love their versatility and speed of preparation – they can be poached, braised, steamed or added to soups and stir-fries.

bok choy

A mildly flavoured green vegetable, also known as Chinese chard or Chinese white cabbage. Baby bok choy can be cooked whole after washing. If using the larger type, separate the leaves and trim the white stalks. Limit the cooking time so that it stays green and slightly crisp.

choy sum

Also known as Chinese flowering cabbage, this Asian green has small yellow flowers. The green leaves and slender stems are steamed or lightly cooked in stir-fries.

gai larn

Also known as Chinese broccoli or Chinese kale, gai larn is a leafy vegetable with dark green leaves, small white flowers and stout stems (the part of the plant that is most often eaten). Wash thoroughly then steam, braise, boil or stir-fry.

basic bolognese sauce

2 teaspoons olive oil
2 cloves garlic, chopped
2 onions, chopped
1kg (2¼ lb) minced beef
2 x 400g (14 oz) cans tomato puree
1 cup (250ml/8 fl oz) beef stock
¼ cup chopped flat-leaf parsley leaves
sea salt and cracked black pepper
Heat a deep frying pan or saucepan over high heat. Add the oil, garlic and onion and cook for 3 minutes or until just soft.

Add the mince and cook, stirring, until brown. Add the tomato puree and stock and rapidly simmer for 10–15 minutes or until thickened to your liking. Stir through the parsley, salt and pepper. Serves 4.

basic tomato sauce

2 teaspoons olive oil
2 cloves garlic, chopped
1 onion, chopped
2 x 400g (14 oz) cans crushed tomatoes
3 teaspoons sugar
¼ cup chopped basil leaves
Heat a large saucepan over medium heat. Add the oil, garlic and onion and cook for 4–5 minutes or until the onion is tender. Add the tomatoes, sugar and basil, reduce heat and simmer for 10–12 minutes or until thick and pulpy.

capers

Capers are the small, olive green flower buds of the caper bush. Available packed either in brine or salt. Use salt-packed capers when possible, as the texture is firmer and the flavour superior. Before use, rinse thoroughly, drain and pat dry.

cheese

A nutritious food made by curdling the milk of cows, goats, sheep and other mammals using rennet and acidic cultures. Some cheeses have moulds on the outer rind or throughout the whole product.

fetta

Made from goat's, sheep's or cow's milk, fetta is a salty, crumbly cheese which is often stored in brine to extend its shelf life.

goat's cheese and curd

Goat's milk has a characteristic tart flavour, so cheese made from it, sometimes labelled chèvre, has a sharp, slightly acidic taste. Immature goat's cheese is milder and creamier than mature cheese and is sometimes labelled goat's curd.

mascarpone

A fresh Italian triple-cream curd-style cheese. It has a similar consistency to thick (double) cream and is often used in the same way. Available in tubs from specialty food stores and many delicatessens and supermarkets.

parmesan

Italy's favourite hard, granular cheese is made from cow's milk. Parmigiano reggiano is the "Rolls Royce" variety, made under strict guidelines in the Emilia-Romagna region and aged for an average of two years. Grana padano mainly comes from Lombardy and is aged for 15 months.

ricotta

A creamy, finely grained white cheese. Ricotta means "recooked" in Italian, a reference to the way the cheese is produced by heating the whey left over from making other cheese varieties. It's fresh and creamy and low in fat.

chilli tomato sauce

2 teaspoons olive oil
1 onion, chopped
2 small red chillies, seeded and chopped
2 cloves garlic, finely chopped
¼ cup (60ml/2 fl oz) white wine
2 x 400g (14 oz) cans crushed tomatoes
2 tablespoons chopped flat-leaf
    parsley leaves
Heat the oil in a saucepan over medium heat. Add the onion and cook for 5 minutes or until soft and golden. Add the chilli and garlic and cook for a further

minute. Add the wine, crushed tomatoes and chopped parsley and simmer for 5–6 minutes or until the sauce is reduced and slightly thickened.

Chinese barbecued duck

Crispy skinned, spiced and barbecued duck prepared in the traditional Chinese style is available from Chinese barbecue shops and some Asian food stores.

Chinese five-spice powder

This combination of cinnamon, Sichuan pepper, star anise, clove and fennel is available from Asian food stores and most supermarkets.

Chinese rice wine

Similar to dry sherry, Chinese cooking wine is a blend of glutinous rice, millet, a special yeast and the local spring waters of Shao Hsing, where it is made, in northern China. It is sold in Asian supermarkets, often labelled "shao hsing".

coconut cream

The cream that rises to the top after the first pressing of fresh coconut milk, coconut cream is a rich, sweet liquid which is both higher in energy and fat than regular coconut milk. Sold in cans at the supermarket. Light (low-fat) versions are also available.

coconut dressing

¾ cup (185ml/6 fl oz) coconut milk
1 tablespoon finely grated ginger
1 garlic clove, crushed
sea salt

Place the coconut milk, ginger, garlic and salt in a small saucepan over medium heat and cook for 5 minutes or until the dressing is warmed through.

coconut milk

A milky sweet white liquid made by soaking grated fresh coconut flesh or desiccated coconut in warm water and squeezing through muslin or cheesecloth to extract the liquid. Available in cans or freeze-dried from supermarkets, coconut milk should not be confused with coconut juice, which is a clear liquid from the inside of young coconuts.

cucumber noodle salad

150g (5¼ oz) dried rice vermicelli noodles
2 Lebanese cucumbers, sliced
4 stalks celery, finely sliced
100g (3½ oz) lettuce leaves

Place the noodles in a bowl, cover with boiling water and soak for 6–8 minutes or until tender. Drain and rinse under cold water. Place the cucumbers, celery and lettuce leaves in a medium bowl and toss with the noodles to combine.

eschalots

A member of the onion family, eschalots are smaller and have a milder flavour than brown, red or white onions. A popular ingredient in Europe, they look like small brown onions with purple-grey tinged skins. Asian shallots are smaller again with pinkish skins and grow in clusters.

fish sauce

An amber-coloured liquid drained from salted, fermented fish and used to add flavour to Thai and Vietnamese dishes. Available from supermarkets and Asian food stores, this pungent sauce is often labelled "nam pla".

hoisin sauce

A thick, sweet Chinese sauce made from fermented soybeans, sugar, salt and red rice. Used as a dipping sauce or marinade and as the sauce for Peking duck, hoisin is available from most supermarkets.

kaffir lime leaves

Fragrant leaves with a distinctive double leaf structure, used crushed or shredded in Thai dishes. Available fresh or dried from Asian food stores and greengrocers.

kecap manis

Sometimes labelled ketjap manis, this is a very thick and sweet but salty Indonesian soy sauce used as a condiment or dipping sauce. Available from Asian food stores.

lemon caper salsa

1 tablespoon olive oil
30g (1 oz) butter
1 clove garlic, crushed
4 green onions (scallions), chopped
1½ tablespoons salted capers, rinsed and drained
1 tablespoon lemon juice
1 tablespoon lemon zest

Heat the oil and butter in a non-stick frying pan over medium heat. Add the garlic, onions, capers, lemon juice and zest. Cook for 1 minute.

lemongrass

A tall, lemon-scented grass used in Asian cooking, and particularly in Thai dishes. Peel away the outer leaves and chop the tender root-end finely, or add in large pieces during cooking and remove before serving. Available from Asian food stores and some greengrocers.

mushrooms

The fruiting bodies of spore-bearing fungi, cultivated year-round. Wild mushrooms are an autumn speciality.

button

This tender little mushroom tightly closed around its stalk is the young form of the commercial field mushroom. White and mildly flavoured, it can be used raw in salads, but is tastier when cooked in stews, stir-fries and pasta sauces.

oyster

This shell-shaped mushroom, sometimes called abalone, has a delicate flavour and tender bite. Colours range from pearly white to apricot-pink. Tear rather than cut and cook gently, whether simmering in soups, pan-frying, or grilling. When eaten raw, they can trigger an allergic response.

porcini

Available fresh in Europe and the UK and sold dried elsewhere, including Australia and the US. They have an almost meaty texture and earthy taste. Soak dried porcini mushrooms before using, and use the soaking liquid if desired.

portobello

This large, flat mushroom is closed related to the white field mushroom but has a nutty, brown colour, flaky skin and richer flavour. A mature version of the Swiss brown, its meaty texture makes it suitable for robust cooking styles.

shiitake

A tan to dark brown mushroom with a meaty texture and rich earthy taste akin to wild mushrooms. Its dried form, found in Asian food stores, gives the most intense flavour. Use in stir-fries, risottos or slow-cooked dishes.

Swiss brown

A button version of the portobello, and a more flavoursome substitute for the common white button mushroom. Use in pasta sauces, risottos or braises.

mustard dressing

2 very fresh eggs
2 tablespoons Dijon mustard
⅓ cup (80ml/2½ fl oz) lemon juice
sea salt and cracked black pepper
⅔ cup (165ml/5 fl oz) vegetable oil
½ cup chopped basil
Process the eggs, mustard, lemon juice, salt and pepper in a food processor or blender. With the motor running, slowly pour in the vegetable oil. Stir in the basil.

nori

Thin sheets of dried, vitamin-packed seaweed used in Japanese-style dishes and to wrap sushi. Available in packets from some supermarkets and Asian stores.

pancetta

A cured and rolled Italian-style meat that is like prosciutto but less salty and with a softer texture. It's sold in chunks or thinly sliced and can be eaten uncooked.

prosciutto

Italian ham that has been salted and air-dried for up to two years. The paper-thin slices are eaten raw or used to flavour cooked dishes. Often used to wrap figs or melon as part of an antipasto platter.

rice vinegar

Made from fermenting rice or rice wine, rice vinegar is milder and sweeter than vinegars made by oxidising distilled alcohol or wine made from grapes. Rice wine vinegar is available in white (colourless to pale yellow), black and red varieties from Asian food stores.

sashimi-grade tuna

Sashimi-grade means the freshest fish available. They are line-caught and, therefore, have no bruises. It's best to buy a centre piece from the fillet as it won't have veins, skin or blood lines. To ensure freshness, you should buy your fish from the market on the day you're going to eat it.

sweet chilli sauce

This popular dipping and stir-fry sauce is a bottled condiment made from sugar, chopped chillies, vinegar and salt. Available from supermarkets and Asian food stores.

Thai basil

Thai basil is a tropical strain of basil and is common in South-East Asian cooking. It has anise overtones to the basil flavour, and has small, dark green leaves with purple stems and flowers. Whole leaves are added to Thai curries, stir-fries, salads and soups. Thai basil, sometimes referred to as holy basil, is available from Asian supermarkets and most green grocers.

tofu

Literally translated as "bean curd", tofu is a high-protein food popular across Asia. Made by coagulating the milk of soy beans, and pressing the curd into blocks, tofu comes in several grades according to the amount of moisture which has been removed. Silken tofu is the softest, with a custard or junket-like texture. Soft tofu is slightly firmer with the texture of raw meat, while dried or firm tofu has the texture of, and cuts like, a semi-hard cheese such as haloumi or paneer. Usually sold packed in water from the refrigerated section of supermarkets and Asian food stores. You can also buy packaged deep-fried tofu.

veal ragout

8 x 200g (7 oz) veal osso bucco
sea salt and cracked black pepper
flour, for dusting
3 tablespoons olive oil
3 garlic cloves, sliced
6 eschalots, peeled and halved
1 tablespoon tomato paste
½ cup (125ml/4 fl oz) red wine
400g (14 oz) can chopped tomatoes
1 cup (250ml/8 fl oz) tomato puree
2 cups (500ml/16 fl oz) beef stock
2 oregano sprigs
500g (1 lb) button mushrooms, halved

Sprinkle the veal with salt and pepper
and dust with flour. Heat a large shallow
saucepan over high heat. Add the oil and
cook the veal in batches for 2–3 minutes
each side or until well browned. Remove
from the pan. Add the garlic and eschalots
to the pan and cook for 1 minute. Return
the veal to the pan, add the tomato paste
and wine and cook, stirring, for 1 minute.
Add the tomatoes, tomato puree, stock
and oregano. Bring to the boil, reduce
the heat to low, cover and simmer for
50 minutes or until the meat starts to
fall away from the bone. Remove the veal
from the pan, carefully remove the rest
of the meat from the bone and return the
meat to the pan. Add the mushrooms
and cook for a further 30 minutes.

wasabi paste

Wasabi is a very hot Japanese horseradish
paste used in making sushi and as a
condiment. Available from most Asian
food stores and supermarkets.

conversion chart

1 teaspoon = 5ml
1 Australian tablespoon = 20ml (4 teaspoons)
1 UK tablespoon = 15ml (3 teaspoons/½ fl oz)
1 cup = 250ml (8 fl oz)

liquid conversions

metric	imperial	cups
30ml	1 fl oz	⅛ cup
60ml	2 fl oz	¼ cup
80ml	2½ fl oz	⅓ cup
125ml	4 fl oz	½ cup
185ml	6 fl oz	¾ cup
250ml	8 fl oz	1 cup
375ml	12 fl oz	1½ cups
500ml	16 fl oz	2 cups
625ml	20 fl oz	2½ cups
750ml	24 fl oz	3 cups
1 litre	32 fl oz	4 cups

cup measures

1 cup almond meal	110g	3¾ oz
1 cup plain (all-purpose) flour	150g	5¼ oz
1 cup brown sugar	175g	6 oz
1 cup caster (superfine) sugar	220g	7¾ oz
1 cup white sugar	220g	7¾ oz
1 cup arborio rice, uncooked	220g	7¾ oz
1 cup basil leaves	45g	1⅔ oz
1 cup coriander (cilantro) leaves	40g	1½ oz
1 cup mint leaves	35g	1¼ oz
1 cup flat-leaf parsley leaves	40g	1½ oz
1 cup olives	175g	6 oz
1 cup parmesan cheese, finely grated	100g	3½ oz
1 cup green peas, frozen	170g	5⅞ oz

a

absorption method for rice 18
Asian noodle soup with pork 78

b

baked pasta, spinach + ricotta 34
baked risotto 20
    pancetta + sweet potato 50
    pea + pancetta 58
    with pumpkin + fetta 54
barbecued duck with egg noodles 74
beef
    coconut noodles 74
    lime + cucumber noodle salad 82
beetroot + cheese pasta 26
bok choy + noodle stir-fry 78
bolognese sauce 88
broccoli, buttered, with pasta 42
brown rice + herb salad 58

c

caramelised beetroot + cheese pasta 26
carbonara, fettucine 42
cheese + caramelised beetroot pasta 26
chicken
    lemon + herb pilaf 64
    lime + coconut rice 62
    + rice pot 54
    spaghetti salad 34
    spicy Thai soup 78
    Thai lime + lemongrass 82
chilli
    pork + egg noodle soup 70
    tomato sauce 88
chorizo + tomato pasta 30
clam (vongole) pasta 38
coconut
    beef noodles 74
    creamy dressing 62
    dressing 89

    + lime chicken rice 62
combination rice noodles 84
cooking
    dry noodles 17
    dry pasta 16
    fresh noodles 17
    fresh pasta 16
    rice, absorption method 18
cucumber noodle salad 89

d

dressing
    coconut 89
    creamy coconut 62
    mustard 90
    sesame 84
    see also sauces
duck
    barbecued, with egg noodles 74
    + chilli noodle salad 82

e

egg noodle soup with chilli pork 70
eggplant + chilli pasta 26

f

fennel, pea + mint spaghetti 42
fettuccine
    carbonara 42
    winter greens + pancetta 38
five-spice pork fried rice 54
fried rice
    five-spice pork 54
    Thai 50
    vegetable + egg 50

g

garlic prawn + lemon pasta 26
ginger pork noodle stir-fry 82
green tea soba noodles with vegetables 70

l

laksa, vegetable 78
lamb
    with black bean + garlic sauce 70
    with nut-spiced pilaf + cumin 62
lasagne 44
lemon
    caper salsa 89
    + garlic prawn pasta 26
    + herb chicken pilaf 64
lime
    beef + cucumber noodle salad 82
    + coconut chicken rice 62

m

meatballs + spaghetti 44
mixed mushroom risotto 64
mushroom
    risotto 64
    + thyme creamy pasta 34
mustard dressing 90

n

noodle salad with crisp tofu 84
noodles 66–85
    cooking 17
nut-spiced pilaf + cumin lamb 62

o

omelette, crispy rice 58

p

paella, prawn 58
pancetta
    + sweet potato baked risotto 50
    white bean + rosemary spaghetti 30
    + winter greens fettuccine 38
parmesan risotto balls 50
pasta 22–45
    with buttered broccoli 42

cooking 16

with prosciutto, ricotta + peas 34

pea

fennel + mint spaghetti 42

+ pancetta baked risotto 58

prosciutto + ricotta pasta 34

pesto pasta 26

pilaf

lemon + herb chicken 64

nut-spiced with cumin lamb 62

pork

Asian noodle soup 78

chilli + egg noodle soup 70

five-spiced, with fried rice 54

ginger noodle stir-fry 82

Thai with noodles 74

prawn

garlic + lemon pasta 26

noodle soup 70

paella 58

prosciutto, ricotta + pea pasta 34

pumpkin + sage brown butter pasta 38

r

ragout

veal 91

veal pasta 30

rice 46–65

cooking 18

+ herb salad 58

for sushi 21

risotto

mixed mushroom 64

parmesan balls 50

stirred 19

risotto (baked) 20

pancetta + sweet potato 50

pea + pancetta 58

pumpkin + fetta 54

roasted eggplant + chilli pasta 26

S

sage + brown butter pasta 30

salad

brown rice + herb 58

chicken spaghetti 34

cucumber noodle 89

lime beef + cucumber noodle 82

noodle with crisp tofu 84

shredded duck + chilli noodle 82

salmon, wasabi-crusted with rice noodles 74

salsa, lemon caper 89

sauce

basic bolognese 88

basic tomato 88

chilli tomato 88

white 44

sesame dressing 84

smoked trout, caper + ricotta spaghetti 38

soba noodles with vegetables 70

soup

Asian noodle with pork 78

egg noodle with chilli pork 70

prawn noodle 70

spicy Thai chicken 78

soy chicken + rice pot 54

spaghetti

chicken salad 34

+ meatballs 44

pea, fennel + mint 42

smoked trout, caper + ricotta 38

with tomatoes + capers 42

white bean, rosemary + pancetta 30

spicy Thai chicken soup 78

spinach + ricotta baked pasta 34

stir-fry

bok choy + noodle 78

ginger pork noodle 82

sushi

cut-out 62

lettuce-cup 62

rice 21

simple eggcup 54

t

Thai

chicken soup 78

fried rice 50

lime + lemongrass chicken 82

pork with noodles 74

tomato

+ caper spaghetti 42

+ chorizo pasta 30

sauce 88

V

veal

pasta ragout 30

ragout 91

vegetable

+ egg fried rice 50

laksa 78

vongole pasta 38

W

wasabi-crusted salmon with rice noodles 74

white bean, rosemary + pancetta
spaghetti 30

white sauce 44

winter greens + pancetta fettuccine 38

A beautiful collection of clever and simple recipes
from Australia's favourite cookbook author

roast tomato, chickpea and white bean salad

250g (8 oz) cherry tomatoes
400g (14 oz) can chickpeas (garbanzos), rinsed and drained
400g (14 oz) can white beans, rinsed and drained
1 red onion, thinly sliced
2 cups mint leaves
70g (2½ oz) rocket (arugula) leaves
2 tablespoons lemon juice
2 tablespoons olive oil
sea salt and cracked black pepper

Preheat the oven to 200°C (400°F). Place the tomatoes on a baking
tray lined with non-stick baking paper and cook for 5 minutes or until
softened. Place the tomatoes, chickpeas, beans, onion, mint and rocket
in a bowl and toss to combine. To serve, drizzle with the lemon juice
and olive oil and sprinkle with salt and pepper. Serves 4.

recipe taken from *simple essentials: salads + vegetables*

donna hay
SIMPLE ESSENTIALS

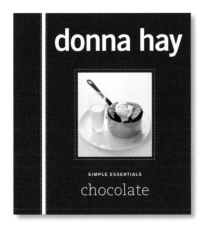

donna hay

SIMPLE ESSENTIALS
chocolate

donna hay

SIMPLE ESSENTIALS
salads + vegetables

donna hay

SIMPLE ESSENTIALS
pasta, rice + noodles

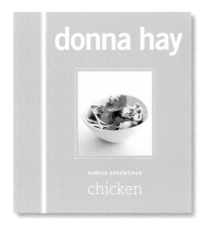

donna hay

SIMPLE ESSENTIALS
chicken

donna hay

SIMPLE ESSENTIALS
fruit

donna hay

SIMPLE ESSENTIALS
beef, lamb + pork

Available now from all booksellers

At the age of eight, Donna Hay put on an apron and never looked back. She completed formal training in home economics at technical college then moved to the world of magazine test kitchens and publishing where she established her trademark style of simple, smart and seasonal recipes all beautifully put together and photographed. It is food for every cook, every food lover, every day and every occasion. Her unique style turned her into an international food publishing phenomenon as a bestselling author, publisher of *donna hay magazine*, newspaper columnist, and creator of a homewares and food range.

books by Donna Hay: *off the shelf, modern classics book 1, modern classics book 2, the instant cook, instant entertaining, simple essentials: chicken, simple essentials: chocolate, simple essentials: salads + vegetables, simple essentials: fruit, simple essentials: beef, lamb + pork*, plus more.